Who Taught You About Money?

Thanks for reading
and learning about
money!

4/24/2014

Other books by Richard Harris:

If I Had a Penny . . .

I'm Walking, I'm Running, I'm Jumping, I'm Hopping . . .

Who Taught You About Money?

A FUN BOOK FOR YOUNG PEOPLE

Richard Harris

Illustrated by Charlotte Marriott

HAMPTON ROADS
PUBLISHING COMPANY, INC.

for the evolving human spirit

To my wife, Carol, for all of her love, encouragement,
and support for this project.

A special thanks to Fred Bateman, Warren Aleck, Dan Ryan,
Jeff Scott, and Brad Cox, whose enthusiasm and input
have been helpful in bringing this book to fruition.

Hampton Roads Publishing Company, Inc.
1125 Stoney Ridge Road
Charlottesville, VA 22902

434-296-2772
fax: 434-296-5096
www.hrpub.com

If you are unable to order this book from your local bookseller, you may order
directly from the publisher. Quantity discounts for organizations are available.
Call 1-800-766-8009.
ISBN 1-878901-91-5
Printed on acid-free paper in China

Hi, I'm Banker Sawbuck* and this is my book.
Please don't stop here . . . go ahead, take a look.
The book looks at ideas that are sometimes confusing
And helps make them simpler and perhaps somewhat amusing.
Who Taught You About Money? hopes to stimulate thought,
So you get your money's worth from this book that you bought.
Now, find a good light and a comfortable chair
And you turn the pages and I'll take it from there.
When you finish the book, you'll know some new things, for sure.
Review them, renew them, and they'll surely endure.

*Sawbuck: a. A sawhorse: b. Slang—A ten-dollar bill.
(*Webster's New Collegiate Dictionary*, G. & C. Merriam Co. [1956], p. 752.)

WHAT IS MONEY?

Money, what is it?
How much do we need?

Some of it's green.
Does it come from a seed?

Some's made of metal.
Does it come from rocks?

I've heard time is money.
Does it come from clocks?

The answer seems simple, 'cause all that I've had
has come from my grandfolks or my mom or my dad.

But let's stop all this guessin', let's stop all this chatter
and try to find someone to help solve this matter.

Hmm . . . could it come from a greenhouse? That seems to make sense.
Or could it be candy; I've heard of money from mints?

Let's talk to the banker; I've heard that he's funny.
But, I would be too if I had his money.

Say hey, Mr. Sawbucks (Banker). I've got a question. I'll read it,
"Where does money come from and why do we need it?"

Does money come from seeds or greenhouses or clocks?
Should we keep it in a bank or stuff it in our socks?

Said Mr. Sawbucks (the Banker), "I see how it's all quite confusing.
But your questions to me are downright amusing.

There'll be no guarantees, but I'll do what I can, sir,
to humbly consider and supply the right answer."

Money began when the items we traded,
became too hard to carry or to store or they faded.

You see, if I had some sheep
and you had some goats
and Danny had denim,
and Olive had oats,

And you wanted sheep, and I
wanted oats,
and Olive the denim, but no
one wanted goats.

Then regardless of how many swaps that were made,
you would be holding the goats left to trade.

You know from the past that the goats will go,
but will they go quickly or will they go slow?

So what can I keep 'til the goats can be sold
that won't waste and won't rot and won't ever grow old?

Money's the answer, yes money's the thing—
a symbol of value to paupers and kings.

Some paper or coins that represent *value*
to buy things or save it, please hear what I tell you.

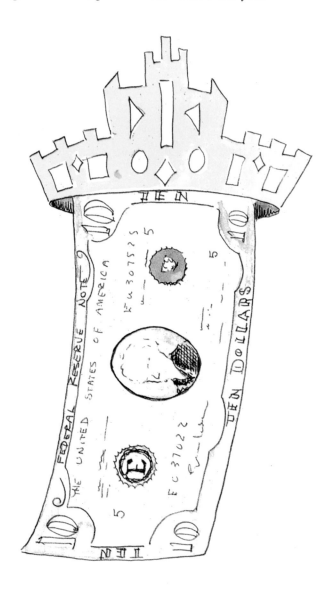

KNOWLEDGE OF MONEY

Who taught you about birds and about bees making honey?
Who taught you all that you know about money?

Who taught you about families and what parents should do?
Who taught you about love? Who taught you about you?

How did you learn to make a decision?
Or not to tell lies? Or turn on television?

The source of much knowledge we find in our schools.
And in churches and homes we learn of life's rules.

We learn quite a lot from our friends, good and bad,
and one-on-one conversation with our mom and dad.

Knowledge will sometimes just fall in your lap,
or perhaps while you're dreaming or taking a nap.

But most knowledge comes when we're seriously seeking,
and some we will lose, like our brain has been leaking.

Learning a new thing you know nothing about
may teach you about something you can't live without.

Seriously seeking and diligently digging
may uncover new things,
like why piggies love pigging.

To learn about money you musn't depend
on learning at school or learning from friends.

Schools just don't teach it and friends may not know.
So, how do you find out? Yes, where do you go?

Start with your parents, ask them to teach you.
Sure, ask them today, I humbly beseech you.

Go to the library, look up Finance and Money,
and talk to a banker, sometimes they're kinda funny.

Seek out and talk to a Certified Financial Planner.
He helps plan about money, he has a real money manner.

Don't be like a mushroom and live in the dark,
you can set knowledge ablaze with one tiny spark!

A Medium OF Exchange

Money is basically a medium of exchange,
paper and coins so it's easy to make change.

Money at its best is a tool that we can use,
money at its worst is a weapon to abuse.

Money by itself is neither good nor is it bad,
it's the way in which you choose to use it that brings joy or makes you sad.

Money when used wrongly has made many man a fool,
but performs, oh so strongly, as a wise man's useful tool.

You can carry money with you or store some of it in banks,
and save it for a rainy day, at which time you could give thanks.

Money is a means of keeping score to some it seems,
some think that they don't have enough until it fills their dreams.

ATTITUDE ABOUT MONEY

"It's not your *aptitude* but your *attitude*
that determines your *altitude* with a little *intestinal fortitude*."

It has been said that "money is the root of all evil," but
it's the "love of money" that's as harmful as a weevil.

Money, like the ocean, must be treated with respect.
"The careless use of money may cause a financial shipwreck."

"Use it or lose it" is a fact regarding muscle,
and also about money, lazy money without hustle.

So, save and invest
some of all that you earn
and never believe
you have "money to burn."

Don't wear yourself out
to get rich, for a season
but read, look, and listen
and learn how to reason.

So be a good *steward* of all that comes to you
and your family and others will be blessed through you.

No matter how smart someone seems to be
with a bad attitude he will never be free

to soar like the eagle to incredible heights
and feel good about himself and sleep through the nights.

Let your attitude show courage, be consistent, stick to it.
Don't worry, don't hurry, make your mind up. "Just do it!"

FIVE USES OF MONEY

There're basically only five uses for money,
four kinda fun, but one not so funny.

You can *give it* or *spend it* or *save* or *invest*,
but first you pay *taxes*, then split up the rest.

You see, governments have gotta have money to run,
so we all pay *taxes* to have basic things done.

Then you decide how much you will *give*
then how much to *spend* in order to live.

Saving is short term storage of money,
a *put and take* proposition, like bees do with honey.

To *invest* you *put and hold* over time,
and watch how a *dollar* can grow from a *dime*!

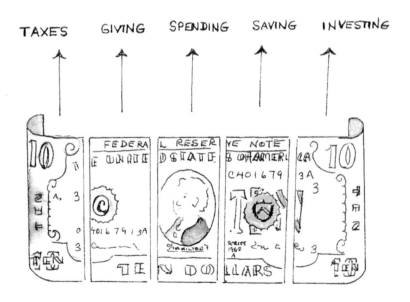

TAXES

There are some things we need to live everyday
but they cost so much that there's no way to pay.

Like military ships and planes for defense
and health care for old folks . . . that seems to make sense;

Like quality education and disposing of trash,
things we all want but don't have the cash.

Now, here's an idea
with just the right touch,
"If everyone pays a little,
no one pays too much!"

Just as surgeons need scalpels
and woodmen need axes,
and bakers need dough,
the government needs taxes.

To pay for the services
that benefit us all,
taxes come in all sizes,
some *BIG*, others *small*.

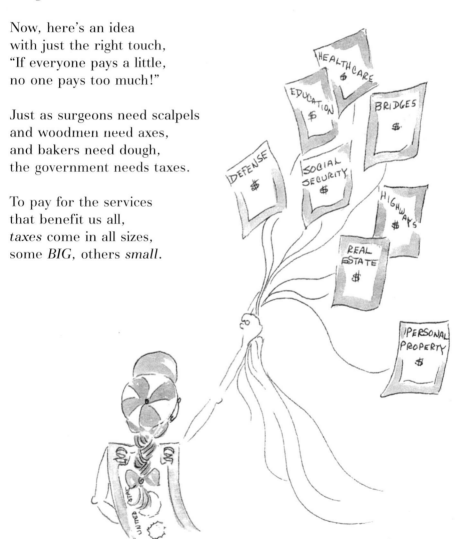

Uncle Sam taxes income and accumulated wealth
and *social security tax* for retirement and health.

States tax us, too, to provide education,
build bridges and highways with periodic rest stations.

Cities *tax* real estate and other property you own,
soon, the hard facts are a yard tax and a dog tax on bones!

There are two systems of tax in the U.S. of A.
and the one that you use determines how much you pay.

One system of tax is for the *informed*
like cavemen who got cold, built a fire and were warmed.

The other tax system is for those who don't know
who might plant a tadpole and expect a frog to grow.

Those who are informed pay less money in taxes
than the one who doesn't know and simply relaxes.

Pay less tax, save more dough, and your assets will grow.
Pay more tax, save less cash, and the assets will go!

GIVING

Some folks have more funds than they need just to live
and decide they will share, yes, decide they will give.

Giving and sharing is living and caring.
You can give away toys or perhaps clothes you're not wearing.

You can give away money or time of you please
to support your house of worship or to fight a disease.

The government knows that to give is quite good
and lowers the taxes on people who would.

We're always surrounded by folks who have not,
but if everyone gives a little, no one has to give a lot.

But do you give? How much and to whom?
What about the United Way or the Lions Club selling brooms?

Find something you believe in, then give from the heart.
Ten percent of your earnings is a good place to start.

But when everything is said and done,
when you give it away it is surely gone.

Whether you give money or time or things that you own,
give cheerfully, please, don't complain and don't moan;

Your gifts will return at a time most surprising
and give you a view of a few new horizons.

LIFESTYLE

Life's about living and *style's* about how you do it.
Everyone has a *lifestyle* and wants to improve it.

Lifestyle depends on how much you learn
about making choices and spending the money you earn.

You can choose a high lifestyle, enjoy life's "finer things"
and cover yourself with jewelry and rings.

Or, choose a low lifestyle with none of life's frills,
get up, go to work, make a buck, and pay your bills.

A sensible choice might be somewhere between,
in a word, "moderation," a lifestyle that's lean.

You see, when you spend a dollar you lose it forever.
But saving a dollar shows the world that you're clever.

When you choose to save it, you have future choices
and get to hear clearly those "attaboy" voices.

SAVINGS

When taxes are paid and you've given your BEST,
and your lifestyle is paid for, what do you do with the REST?

Save for the short term, for things you might need,
but don't have the money, please listen, take heed.

Save for a *margin* that will last half a year,
in case things don't go well, to see your way clear.

Savings can help you weather financial storms
and welcome the sunrise on a beach that it warms.

Savings are dollars you must set apart
to create a margin, to ensure a good start.

When you save money, you hold it a while
for things unexpected or to enhance your lifestyle.

So, you put and you take as the need may arise
but, replace what you take and you'll prove you are wise.

Save for a TV or to install a pool
or take a vacation but don't be a fool!

Save for the bad times and good times as well,
'cause emergencies and opportunities come at times you can't tell.

INVESTING

Investing is putting money away over time.
A "put and hold" kinda habit that will cause your *assets* to climb.

Once you have savings that will last half a year,
you begin to invest, yes, the way will be clear.

You see, investing requires that you *risk* or take chances,
which might cause some loss but it usually enhances.

The money you have will grow over time.
Then your money makes money, now that can't be a crime!

You see, when money makes money it always is working,
all day and all night like coffee that's perking.

It never gets tired, it never needs rest.
Having money that's working is simply the best!

Now, the risk that you take can be smaller or greater,
as small as a pinhead or as great as a crater!

The higher the risk, the more your money will earn,
and what you get back is known as return.

It doesn't make sense to risk all of your money;
'cause when you risk you might lose and that's really not funny.

So, you *invest* some that is *safe*, but the *return* is low,
and *invest* some with *slight risk* so your *income* will grow.

And some you *invest* that will *grow* somewhat *faster*,
a little more risk shouldn't end in a disaster.
The basic idea is to spread risk around,
"slow risk" and "grow risk," but keep your feet on the ground.

And when you are tempted, don't give in to your cravings.
Always keep your investments apart from your savings.

BUDGET

You need to keep track of how your money flows,
where does it come from and then where it goes.

To spend more than you earn just doesn't make sense,
when you're out of money, it makes you feel tense.

So spend less than your income and don't try to fudge it,
spend less than you make, learn early to budget.

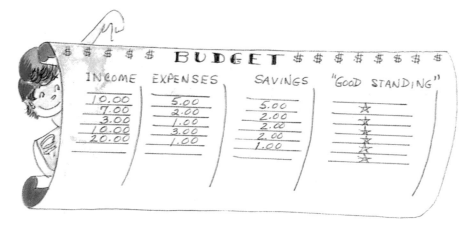

Make note of *all* of your incoming money,
then note where it goes, please, don't be a dummy.

A budget tracks income and expenses for planning,
and helps you maintain financial good standing.

Income can be from the wages you earn
or your money making money, yes, investment return.

And sometimes your income can come from a gift,
and jack up your savings, yes, a financial lift!

Then pay taxes and give some and pay obligations
and save some, invest some, but track destinations.

Know where it comes from and know where it is going,
be smart, keep a chart of how your dollars are flowing!

BANK

Sometimes you have more money than is needed right away
and you need a place to park it for a rainy night or day.

Some place you know is safe and when you want it you can have it,
and will even pay you "rent," if you choose that place to save it.

To whomever had the idea, we give special thanks,
there are places safe to park it, special places known as *banks*.

There are big banks, there are small banks and some banks in between.
There are short banks, there are tall banks, many banks you've never seen!

What do banks do but pay you interest on the money that you're parking?
Do they tell you they will help you quiet your dog when he is barking?

No, banks are like stations or terminals for money,
like the nest is for bird eggs, like the hive is for honey.

When you save it, you *bank* it for use sometime later,
to take a *trip*, buy a *car*, or buy *shoes* made of alligator!

Suppose I need something but my money is lacking,
and I go to the banker and ask for his backing.

Show no sorrow, you can borrow bucks to get the things you need,
if you prove you can repay it and your *credit's* up to speed.

Bees make honey, banks loan money and how sweet they both can be.
Don't take too much, and use them with responsibility.

GOALS

As we live our lives, we need some direction
and from time to time make mid-course corrections.

If you're just not sure in what direction you're going
any road will take you and you'll arrive without knowing.

So, we're taught to set targets or goals, so they're called,
things we can aim for to avoid getting stalled.

Goals help us make progress and measure results
and apply to all children as well as adults.

Goals can be *short term* like finding a job for the summer
or *long term;* go to college so life won't be a bummer.

Goals can be fun goals, like planning a vacation
or, perhaps goals can be grown-up, like building a space station.

Whatever the goal, the benefits can be substantial
and you might even decide to have goals that are *financial.*

Financial goals are goals that concern your money
like saving for a "rainy day" on the days that are "sunny."

A sunny day's a good day when you're in control,
a rainy day's a rough day like when your boat's full of holes.

Financial goals are tools for financial direction
that in turn help provide future financial protection.

One important task to insure goals will help you
is to write them, don't fight them, please hear what I tell you.

When they're written, you can read them and they're sure to last longer;
then review them, bite and chew them, and they're sure to grow stronger.

EARNINGS

Some people say they have "money to burn."
That must not be money that they had to earn!

Earnings are the *money* you receive for the *time*
you work at a job . . . like police solving crimes.

Wages are paid for what we do and we know,
like repairing computers or directing a show.

The higher the skill, the higher the wage,
this can be true regardless of age.

The higher wages go to those who've been schooled
and rulers seem to earn more then those who are ruled.

Some jobs are set up to pay an hourly wage,
like $10.00 per hour for building a stage.

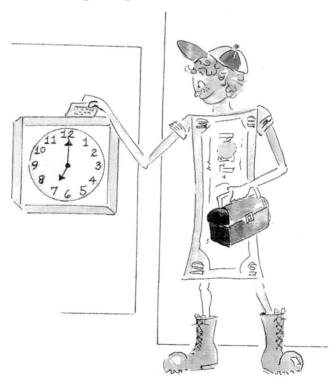

Some jobs are set up to pay a straight *salary*,
like $20,000 per year to run an art gallery.

Sometimes *extra effort*, like a strong wind that's blown us,
will provide a financial windfall, when you're paid a *bonus*.

Perhaps a job as a salesperson will be your decision,
your pay is a percent of your sales, known as a *commission*.

Example: Sales = $10,000
Commissions %   .05
                  $500.00   = commission

To earn a good wage surely makes sense,
but never at someone else's expense.

DEBT

Say hey, Mr. Sawbuck, before we forget,
would you kindly explain the concept of *debt*?

I'm glad that you asked, little friends of mine,
it's not very good, but a sign of the times.

Some things that we buy cost more than we have,
and it would take much too long it we waited to save.

So, make a *down payment*, pay the rest in the future,
buy now, pay later, on terms that will suit you.

To buy now, pay later can be kinda good,
as long as we buy the things that we should.

Don't buy now, pay later for things that lose value,
please, listen close to the words that I tell you.

When things that you buy become worth more than you pay,
it's okay to buy now, then pay on the way.

As you repay what you owe, try hard not to forget,
the amount that you owe is how much you're in *debt*!

Taxes and *giving* and *lifestyle*, all three
should be paid out of income that leaves you *debt free*!

Don't borrow to buy things you tend to forget,
and you can't remember the source of your debt.

You'll have people tell you, "Use plastic, don't sweat it!"
but, be careful don't fall for the crunch we call *credit*!

The fleeting moment of pleasure you gain
may cause you a long-term measure of pain.

You have to *pay back* every dime that you borrow,
plus interest which may cause you financial sorrow.

So, put off buying things that you really don't need
until the money's in hand, you'll be happy indeed!

DEBT FREE!

A financial goal for both you and me
could be or should be that we are *debt free*.

To be free of debt and owe no one a dime
will be as sweet as a limeade and you own the lime.

(To be free of debt and own no one a cent
will put you more in control of where your money's spent.)

There's one basic fact you should always remember,
the borrower 'til he pays back is slave to the lender.

If you must borrow money to buy something expensive,
make sure what you buy has value that's extensive.

Then set your sight on repaying the money you owe
just as soon as you're able, don't repay it slow.

Do it right, *keep debt light*, and once you're debt free,
you can seize, if you please, a good opportunity.

But when you're strapped or you're trapped and your *cash flow's* near zero,
don't let down, pay your debt and you'll be a hero.

INTEREST

Sometimes you need money you simply don't have
to buy something for which you've had no means to save.

For just such occasions we all must give thanks,
to the piggy's and the biggy's that invented the banks.

Banks will loan money for needs great and small,
when they feel sure the *borrower* will repay it all.

And, until you repay it, the banks charge you rent.
It's called *interest* or rent on the money they lent.

When you have some money that you want to save,
you have the chance to make the bank your slave.

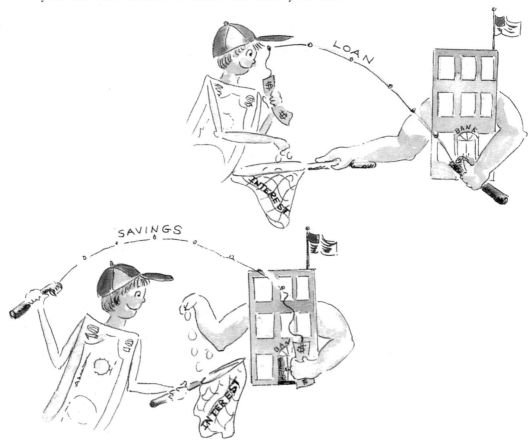

The bank becomes the "borrower" and pays *interest* to you,
and you are the *lender* and slavemaster too.

So, the lesson to learn and the lesson to render,
is that the "borrower is always the slave to the lender."

Interest rates can differ at all different banks,
so, make you a list and check out the ranks.

Interest adds money to the money you owe
and the longer the payback the more it will grow.

Interest you get for the money you lend
can grow and can grow and become a good friend.

When interest you've earned, earns interest of its own,
it's said to *"compound"* and rewards the wisdom you've shown.

Whether it's interest you receive or interest you pay,
interest is working 24 hours each day!

NET WORTH

When you *buy* something it's said that you *own* it.
Let someone else use it, it's said that you *loan* it.

If something you buy could later be sold
it's said to have value and you may choose it to hold.

Things that have value are known as assets, you see,
but the dollars that you owe are *liabilities*.

When you buy an asset and *borrow* money to buy it,
be sure the asset will *grow* or simply don't try it.

The part of the asset that gives you your value
should be more than you borrow, please hear what I tell you!

The liabilities you owe should be *repaid on time*;
limit your liabilities and your assets will climb.

Grow your assets to the sky, keep liabilities down to earth,
and the space that you create is known as *net worth*.

Just add up your assets and subtract what you owe,
what's left is your *net worth* which over time you can grow!

INSURANCE

There are times when our minds are feeling quite frisky
and we decide not to hide but to do something *risky*.

Risk is hard to explain but is truly quite real,
when the chance to lose gets higher, the more anxious you feel.

So, what do you do about risk? What is the answer?
Sawbuck's three choices are *avoid, accept,* or *transfer.*

If you *avoid* risk there aren't many fun things left to do,
you might as well sell everything and live in a shoe!

To *accept* risk *you* own it,
the responsibility's yours
so, be careful in traffic
or in revolving doors.

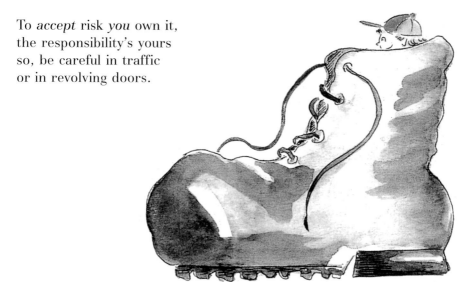

If you *transfer* the risk you may help your endurance,
you let someone else hold the risk when you buy *insurance*.

With pennies you buy dollars for future delivery
to keep you and your household from financial misery.

Insurance provides comfort and protects your finances,
like parachutes to pilots who don't want to take chances.

You can *insure* your house and your car against loss,
and if disaster occurs you don't bear the cost.

You can *insure* your *health* and your *wealth* and your *life*
and keep you and your family from financial strife.

VALUE

A concept of money I've heard of since birth
is the concept of *value*, the concept of worth.

To get more than you paid for is called *value added*
like buying a wood chair, then finding out it's padded.

Value, at best, is quite hard to explain
like the job of a rainbow bidding farewell to the rain.

But when there's no value or value is low,
it makes you feel grumpy, like a car that won't go.

So when you spend money anywhere on this earth,
always seek value, get your money's worth!

KINETIC MONEY

"MONEY ON THE MOVE"

Suppose you could travel, yes, take a long tour,
while looking for something, though just what you're not sure.

You're not at all certain just where you will go . . .
to Paris or Berlin or perhaps Tokyo.

How should you dress . . . hmmm what kind of clothes?
How much money to take, only heaven knows.

Pretend that each place you go has been waiting for you
and you stop at a station and they tell you what to do.

They say your clothes are ready, including your shoes,
just present them your I.D., they're just for you to use.

And money to spend? You'll need some I'm certain,
just step here inside the electronic curtain.

Does this idea sound silly, just doesn't make sense?
The guy who would try should live inside a fence!

Sounds silly you say but, "Hey, wait a minute."
Don't make me a bet 'cause I surely will win it.

I haven't yet figured how to send ahead clothes
but to send ahead money, almost everyone knows.

Electronic tellers, please don't berate them,
almost every big bank has their own ATM.*

Deposit your money before you leave town
and the ATM will simply follow you around.

You must have your card and your own ID number.
Don't leave home without them and try to *remember*.

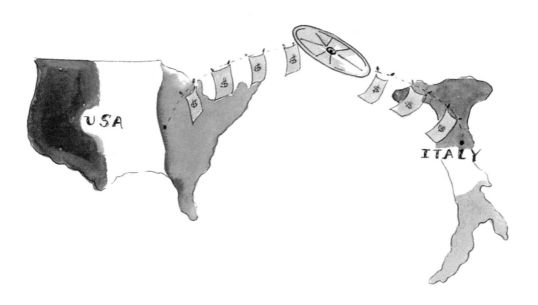

*Automatic Teller Machine

INFLATION

Sometimes things you can't see are truly quite real,
like sheep in a snow storm, or the way that you feel.

One such thing that's a real aggravation
causes things to cost more—it's known as *inflation*.

Inflation, like interest,
is at work all the time,
3–4% each year
it causes prices to climb.

When things people want
are in limited supply,
demand becomes greater
and prices fly high!

Inflation alone
can cause prices to rise
and soon you will see
how much less each dollar buys.

Inflation erodes our "purchasing power"
each dollar buys less with each passing hour.

So, money you invest should beat inflation at least
and then you will tame the *inflation* beast.

SUPPLY AND DEMAND

A basic concept you should understand,
when talking about money, is *supply and demand.*

Supply on the one hand is all that's for sale
on shelves, in warehouses, retail, and wholesale.

Demand, on the other hand is what people want to buy
for which they spend money on things in supply.

When supply is abundant and demand's kinda low,
prices start falling in hope demand will grow.

When demand's on the rise and supply's kinda down,
prices will rise when there's not enough to go around.

When demand meets supply and supply meets demand,
prices are stable, the system works as planned.

Demand's always changing and so are supplies,
sometimes they're down, but other times they rise.

All kinds of things affect demand and may affect supply,
perhaps a bug you cannot see, or perhaps a cloudy sky.

A bug you cannot see, you say? A cloudy sky? Absurd!
How can those change supply and demand? Tell us, give us your word.

A "word" from me is "true" you see and yes you have my word,
bugs and clouds, supply, demand, I agree it sounds absurd.

But suppose a *germ*, a squiggly squirm was discovered in our water.
In the wink of an eye our drinking supply isn't drinkable—doctor's orders!

Demand is still quite strong, you see,
but where is our supply?
The water glass that once was full,
because of bugs, is dry!

OK, Sawbuck, I see "bugs" now,
but clouds present a puzzle.
"A cloud full of rain could put a strain
on orange juice that we guzzle.

Too much rain that fails to drain could flood a grove of oranges,
the crop would shrink, no juice to drink, and the price would be outrageous!

So, there you see how clouds could be harmful to supplies,
I gave my word and now you've heard 'bout germs and cloudy skies."

Capitalism

America is truly the land of the free,
we're surrounded by limitless opportunity.

You can be a banker, a trucker, a doctor, or plumber,
or perhaps a school teacher and be off in the summer.

You can own your own business and accumulate wealth,
or do research in a lab and find cures for ill health.

But first go to school, yes school will open the doors
to a wide world of *options* and the *choice* will be yours.

Two reasons we work are to save and *invest*,
after taxes and giving and spending the rest.

Saving and investing helps accumulate wealth
to help pay for retirement or perhaps failing health.

The more that you save, the more you can *invest*,
build your short term, then long term, and your house will be blessed.

Building wealth is not sinful, it is really quite good,
if you do it the right way and treat folks as you should.

Yes, wealth known as *Capital* is part of the system
of working, saving, and investing known as *Capitalism*.

40

ENTREPRENEURS

Some people create business, they're movers and shakers.
They're willing to take chances, they're proven risk takers.

Where their efforts will take them they're really not sure,
but such is the life of an *entrepreneur*.

They'll take an idea, make it happen, get it started,
and if it doesn't work out they're not brokenhearted.

The entrepreneur's mind is set on *idea creation*
and people of this kind are the backbone of our nation.

The settlers at Jamestown had entrepreneurial drive
and their vision for the future helped to keep it alive.

Even when some said,
"Let's go home, they don't want us!"
an entrepreneur stepped forward
and married Pocahontas.

And old Levi Strauss had an idea
that made sense (cents),
forty-niners, gold miners needed home:
he'd sell them tents!

Tents you say? Oh, not today, it's rugged pants our money buys.
Strauss cut the tents and sewed up pants and put those miners in *Levi's*!

And Henry Ford was seldom bored as he worked on ways to power wheels.
Instead of nappin', he made it happen, now we all drive automobiles.

Now, ideas come to everyone and if you're one that's willing,
then take a chance, like Levi's pants and you might make a million!

FINANCIAL ADVICE

Though money is green, it does not grow on trees
and most that I've had did not come with ease.

Through work and through toil and by the "sweat of the brow"
one day at a time you earn it somehow.

But earning the money is not the whole issue.
What you do with it is the thing that might miss you.

How do you ask the right questions and make the right choices
and not listen to so many "know it all" voices?

How do you know that you're on the right track,
and when making decisions that you have *all* the facts?

The answer's not easy, so please don't be fooled,
it should be someone *you* can talk to who has also been schooled.

Like the friend of a friend or someone you know
and a good rule of thumb is to take it *real slow*.

Check their credentials and references too,
then ask someone you *trust* "just what would *you* do?"

Getting good advice is not all that easy,
but following bad advice can make you feel queasy.

So, just take your time . . . ask some questions then more,
and financial success just might be in store.

ABOUT THE AUTHOR:

Richard Harris is a certified financial planner and former school teacher. He has taught high school financial planning classes for years in an effort to enhance understanding of basic concepts for young people. Richard continues to promote the possibility of teaching basic money or financial concepts on a mandatory basis to middle school and high school students. He believes any subject can be learned better when presented in an interesting, fun-provoking manner.

ABOUT THE ILLUSTRATOR:

Charlotte Marriott is a graduate of William & Mary with a degree in fine arts. She taught art in the Virginia Beach public school system. She has illustrated two books in addition to this one: a children's book, *A Special Day For Nessie* and the Eastern Shore Chapel cookbook, *Holy Chow*.